Why Not to Have Children

-The Full Guide-

With Exclusive Crime Child Zodiac!

By Alexandria Venture

Copyright 2022

Introduction-

Need any additional reasons not to have children? You will find them all here. It is clear that children are a major problem in our lives. Few know how to solve the problems that arise after having children. Our advice is not to have them. However, if you have them, you are lucky enough to have found this instructional book to aid you in how to deal with them. No hate against anyone who is actually a good parent, or has children in general.

Disclaimer

These writings are satirical. While much of what is written is true, the humorous advice in this book is not meant to be followed. Read everything with a grain of salt. You will be able to weed out easily what is factual and what is not. Author and publisher will not be held responsible for any action taken in the advice written in this book. It contains dark humor that is meant for entertainment purposes only. The author themselves would not act upon any ill advice written in this book.

Table of Contents

Expense

The cost of raising a child to age 18 in the year 2022 is estimated at roughly $270,000. (Parker, 2022) If you can afford a child, you should not be complaining about other expenses in your life; as you chose to spend over a quarter million dollars or more on your offspring.

You never hear about the 'joys' of having a child except for those who have had children. 'I wouldn't trade them for anything', you often hear. The reason you only hear this from parents is because they are trying to make the best out of their situation. They are trapped in this lifestyle and are trying to make themselves feel better about what they've gotten themselves into. This is why they always encourage others to have children. Misery likes company. You never hear childless individuals encouraging others to have children.

Would you not rather own your own house for that cost? Or perhaps, if you already have one, an additional house? Such an investment could lead you to an earlier retirement. Now after having children, you may not be able to retire at all. You will slave your entire life away for a human that does not appreciate what you have done for them.

The only reason many can afford to have a child or multiple children is government aid. What happens when that goes away? You will be forced to comply with anything the government and police force instructs you to do, because your financial ability to raise children depends on them. Say hello to governmental slavery. The system has specifically been designed this way.

When holidays approach, the children are conditioned to expect a large amount of gifts. If you choose to comply with such a greedy system, you will put yourself in financial turmoil. The end result is endless want from the child. A reasonable parent would instead give the child one or two simple gifts. This applies to birthdays as well. Parents tend to give their children an oversized amount of gifts and spend far too much money on them. The child is not able to process how much work went into obtaining such things. As a result, their appreciation levels will be low.

Enjoy not being able to be rich or own your dream car. Because after having a child, that's what you signed up for. You will be renting for the rest of your life to a corporate entity or a landowner. You will never be able to truly financially succeed in life if you have a child.

Did you finally land that dream career? Get ready to lose it. Your child has needs and it's your responsibility. If it doesn't force you to quit your job altogether, you will have to leave work early or take days off. This will be highly frowned upon at work. It won't take long for you to be let go.

Unappreciative

Our society has normalized a world where we are vulnerable from all angles. They train the human children to even attack their own parents, and argue even the most valuable of information given.

The school system is a toxic environment. Even their peers alone can easily change a child. It is natural for a subordinate child in a group to immediately succumb to the ways of the group. This is a survival tactic. It has been practiced by humans since the beginning of time. A majority of young humans are bad association. You will quickly discover that your child will begin bucking against what you attempted to train them their entire lives.

As children graduate from infancy, their demonic state will begin to show. They will more often than not abuse other life forms. This includes animals and other children seen as weaker than them. The rise they get out this behavior can also manifest into adulthood. This is why we have adult crime to this day. Parents have to punish the child in an effective manner. Otherwise, apocalyptic results will manifest.

Parents are typically unable to see the 'evil eye' in a hateful child. It can easily be seen by those not of the family. It is because they are blinded by the thought that their bloodline can do no harm. Instead, stay awake and monitor the behavior of the child. You cannot trust them. Why would you choose to live with an untrustworthy and hateful being?

One effective method against school brainwashing is sending your child to a private school. You may also homeschool them. However, if you homeschool them then you may not be able to work a full-time job. This will make the financial situation even worse. Sadly, brainwashing still does exist in private schools. Homeschooling has a better chance of improving their mental state. Private schools are also rather expensive, thus adding an unavoidable expense onto yourself unless you break down and send them to public school. It's your choice- financial hardship or a brainwashed child.

Many adults have a child because they want their legacy to go on. This aspect is a misconception. Many children anymore grow up nothing like their own parents. Not only will they not look like you, they won't act like you, follow your advice or want to have anything to do with you.

Ugly/Hideous

All children look the same. If you took a group of infants (even as little as ten of them), the parents would not be able to successfully identify their own child. They are typically all mostly if not completely bald. Their physical appearance is not attractive at all. It is a wonder that they are allowed to exist.

No one can truthfully say that their child looks good. All parents are biased. Each one says that their own child looks attractive. It is not statistically possible for every child to look proper. The hard facts are that most children are hideous.

Even children themselves are aware of their own ugliness. At a young age they have given up how they appear to the public eye. Visual appearance is a way in the wind to them. Insightful parents can help doctor their child's appearance by placing more clothes on the child. The more of them can be covered, the less hideous the child will appear.

The human body in general has an unfortunate appearance. This also applies to adults. You must admit that we look far more unattractive than a beautiful wild animal. Humans are extremely bald, and formed in an unfortunate manner. Their bodies are formed in a way that we are even unable to survive without tools or community aid. Animals in general are superior.

Hopefully, you don't care about the public opinion of you. Anyone seen with children is seen as weak and careless. With multiple children, you are seen even more as a low-class citizen. Everyone assumes you are a user of the system. Your friends will stop talking to you as well. Nobody wants to be around your loud, nagging, wild offspring. Because let's be honest- it IS in fact loud, nagging and wild because you are too incompetent to train it correctly. (See Incapability chapter)

Your friends will not want to appear the same as you with your children (weak). This is why they will begin to avoid you, especially in public.

A simple fact exists that many are not aware of. Take a look at the superiority of animals vs humans. A child can take an entire year to be able to walk on their own. A baby animal takes minutes. No wonder you are seen as weak when harboring children! Your baggage is helpless. In the wild, both of you would not be able to survive. Humans in general are less capable than animals.

This leads us to a great reason to adopt a pet instead of having a child. That is, if you are able to care for it properly.

Stress

The amount of stress that children cause is immense. No one can deny this. A 2019 study found that parents tend to lose nearly 2 hours of sleep per night. (Webber, 2019) This cuts down on your entire lifespan. You will literally cut off years of your life to sleep loss alone. Why would you torture yourself if you don't have to?

You may think that sending your child to school will cut down with having to deal with their existence; and thus lower your stress. This is not necessarily true. The school system will cause you even more stress. They will demand financial support for certain activities. They will also procure issues; one after the other. Sometimes the problems are related to your child, and other times not. Every moment will have you in regret.

Who enjoys a child asking the same question twenty times in a row? Nobody, obviously. Who enjoys a child ruining your own home and valuables? Nobody. Children are out of control, and you as the parent are required to control them.

This amount of stress forces parents to enter into a state of alcoholism or drug use. They are then able to deal with the immense amount of stress. It is rare to see drug abuse in childless individuals. This is clear evidence that children are the root cause of drug addiction, reduced life expectancy and decrease of health overall.

Do you have an overall calm lifestyle? Hope you're ready for that to go away. Children of all ages will bring with them emotional havoc in your life. They will constantly be screaming, crying or in anger. Their emotional level is so extreme, that there is nothing quite like it. This is why many parents force medications onto their children. They can't handle the natural lifestyle of these horrid, screeching creatures.

Need to take a vacation to take some stress off of you? Think again. The child has so many needs that it will be incredibly rare for you to do so. Even if you are able to coordinate a vacation where someone else can watch it, they will not want to do so for very long. Also, the expense of childcare is extremely high. This will double or triple the cost of your vacation. Meanwhile, you will receive constant phone calls of accidents the child is having and hell it is giving the caretaker. If you're lucky, it won't have an emergency accident to force you to cancel mid-vacation.

If you are in a relationship, you better hope it's a strong one. A perfect relationship can be ruined by a baby/child. Their intrusion will put a heavy strain on your daily lives. They will intervene in your established way of life and destroy it very quickly.

Incapability

An important factor to address is the overall incapability of parents to raise a child. One in thirty-five children in the United States are adopted. (Lifelong Adoptions, n.d.) In the year 2019, nearly 630,000 abortion cases were reported. This is from a study using 49 reporting locations. (Centers for Disease Control and Prevention, 2021) This is undeniable evidence of the number of individuals that don't even want children. Even so, many will still have the children due to their religious beliefs despite not wanting them.

Parents in general are incapable of properly raising their own children. Take for example, the simple aspect of dietary choice. The parent will choose to give the child whatever it wants, despite the level of healthiness. They will claim, "The child will only eat this". Of course, a child will only eat what it wants. This usually consists of candy, carbs, and meat. You have to enforce your parental power in order to get it to eat a proper meal. If it will only eat candy, will you continue to feed it a diet of just candy? Imbeciles.

The author themselves has witnessed an incredible inability of others to parent their own children. This experience has been seen throughout their entire lifetime. The child will wander, or even be in the same room as the parent. Meanwhile, the child seeks out dangerous materials in order to either inflict self-harm, or destroy property. The parent never takes notice. Having children is a large responsibility, that hardly anyone will recognize.

Many parents will also take a liking to dressing their children exactly like prostitutes. It should go without saying, but it doesn't. They will dress them in short, tight pants and scandalous shirts. Such garments would make a grown human blush. They enjoy advertising their own children for solicitation. Perhaps they are awaiting a payout from thirsty predators?

Many medical experiments and procedures are performed to this day. They are sold as proven and effective, when there is no long-term data. Parents will be the first to line up and sign their children into such experiments. It can have short term side effects, but most often has long term side effects. Any medication containing mercury, aluminum, or formaldehyde should not be taken if you consider you or your child a human being. However, the reason many do these things to their children is a quiet attempt to kill the child. Sometimes, it is effective. There are other ways to punish your child. (See Punishment chapter)

The reason most churches exist is due to the childcare and child entertainment services they offer. This is a silent admittance of the parents wanting to get as far away from their own children as possible. If they are not able to use church services for this purpose, they will do whatever they can to pawn off their children on any friends or family members they can.

In prehistoric times, population control was quite popular. If there were too many children, they would simply sacrifice them to the Gods. Children require immense resources in order to survive. Only a limited number of them would be sustainable. In fact, strong evidence suggests they were devoured via cannibalism. Human teeth marks on child bones were prevalent in excavation discoveries. In general, children were always seen as useless baggage. It takes so many years for them to be able to provide any type of service to others. It's no wonder so many children were slaughtered for centuries up until now. Any child with health problems was automatically done away with in order to help the greater good of the group.

Diseased

Children tend to carry quite a few diseases and illnesses. This was witnessed by the author. There was a dinner event, whereas the parent brought a sick child to the restaurant. Fluid was streaming from the nostrils of the creature. An adult human on the other end of the table requested to hold the child. Thus, half of the attendees had to pass the child down to the destination. The author was taxed with also passing the child down the line. For two solid days thereafter, the author was stricken with severe illness. The toilet became their resting place constantly. Food could not be consumed, and anything that had been digested prior was expelled. What a terrible experience. The diseased child could have just been left at home.

It is well-known that children in general tend to be a cesspool of germs. Their natural odor alone is disgusting. Fluids seep from all orifices. The condition is not in any way or form 'cute.' Disease spreads very quickly throughout entire households and public due to children. They will acquire any local sickness and spread it like wildfire. Meanwhile, you will have to live with and take care of the disadvantaged devil.

Children are more inclined to get an illness than adults. (Centers for Disease Control and Prevention, 2020) Their skin is thinner, and they breathe in more air than adults. The temptation to touch unclean surfaces is too great for children. They will roll in their own or others' filth. It is impossible to have a clean household if a child is in it.

Children are the reason for global warming and worldwide crises. They are proven to breathe more air vs their body weight in comparison to adults. The hot air accumulates in the ozone and tears it apart slowly. This is why we have climate change.

Worldwide viruses enjoy harboring themselves in child bodies and traversing to many areas without showing evidence of infection. That solves the mystery of diseases spreading quickly when nobody seems to be infected. The children carry an immense number of germs and diseases at all times. It is best to social distance them for most of their entire lifespan.

Manipulation

For as long as you let them, children will use mind control tactics in order to get their way. Unfortunately, in this period of time it is highly effective. Parents will treat their children like Gods, and thus upon growing older they will still expect to be treated like Gods. This is why we have unruly teenagers expecting to have everything handed to them.

A common manipulation tactic is crying. If their wants are not met, they will begin to cry louder. Weak parents will often rush over to them and attend to the wants of said child. If the child has everything it needs and it insists on crying, consider this method to curb the behavior. Surround the child with megaphones fixated in the room. Whenever it cries, the noise will be multiplied by an extreme degree. They will quickly notice the audible discomfort and correct their behavior.

A child will ensure you are their slave for their entire lifespan if you let them. The simple solution is not to go along with such a system. You must put them in their place. Otherwise, you'll be nothing but a dusty servant in their materialistic eyes.

Another effective control method they use is the Look of Innocence. Reality check- they're not innocent. If they are trying to manipulate you, you shouldn't need any more confirmation to see they are simply using you for their own selfish desires and benefit.

Suicidal

Why are children so attracted to dangerous objects and situations? We all know they are. Even parents will admit to their own child's tendencies. This is an unspoken truth that everyone inherently knows. "But they don't know any better." -Is the common response. If they didn't actually know any better, they would choose dangerous/safe situations randomly. Instead, children selectively partake in harmful activities above safe ones every time.

Every moment of a child's life involves them actively seeking a way to destroy their own life. Eventually, they do grow out of it. In the meantime, you will have a suicidal creature on your hands that you will have to cage or watch at all times so that it may not succeed at its goal. Even child toys are inherently designed to not have sharp objects or removable parts. Much like criminals in prison, they are capable of dissembling the toys and creating weapons out of them.

Some parents will scoff, "But they're just curious". Many individuals are curious, but few are so curious about taking their own life as a child is. For example, if you provide a room full of toys and a room full of weaponry to a child, we all know which room they will choose. The evidence is undeniable.

This leads us to the inevitable question. Why are children so suicidal? Yes, even infants and toddlers. What draws them to the desire of wanting to off themselves? The answer to this question is uncertain. Some speculate that children are in a higher sense of awareness than adults. Perhaps they know more than we do about the state of the earth and wish to rush to the next life hurriedly. Maybe they were born into a body they didn't expect to manifest in, and which to enter another. Or, could they be so evil that their one and only goal is to inflict everlasting pain to their own parents by leaving their own existence? We may never know, as they are unable to communicate properly at their young age. Conveniently, they also experience amnesia from these actions as they age.

Essentially, not having children is doing a favor to the children themselves.

Multiplication

When adulthood is reached, your offspring will be liable to multiply. In some cases, they may even try to do so beforehand. This will cause you to be responsible for even more infants. You thought you were safe just having one? No, they will reproduce. It is never-ending. They will also expect you to aid them even after adulthood.

Some reason that if they have children, it will ensure their care when they become senile. This is not true. Many of the offspring will cut off contact with their parents and family, especially upon their reaching a high age. Parental hatred has become prevalent. Rather than spending hundreds of thousands of dollars on an ungrateful child, you could have put that away for a comfortable retirement. Perhaps even a high-class retirement home if needed.

Grandparents usually encourage their children to have children. This is because they won't have financial or legal responsibility for them. They will not have to care for them, or anything. The grandchildren will merely be an heir to their bloodline without requiring them to do any work. No one should be obligated to have children for any reason.

If you have any children, you must be prepared for them to beg you to take care of their own children after they reach adulthood. Because nobody likes to take care of children. Your own adult children will try to pawn the task onto you.

Some religions encourage reproduction, while others discourage it. The Mormons for example try to have a solid number of five children per household. This aids in religious population. The Jehovah's Witnesses however, discourage population growth. This is to help them survive Armageddon. It is also an admittance that having children makes you weak.

Some individuals will simply reproduce in order to expand their family name. What is a name? It is nothing. Your children will probably grow to be nothing like you anyway. The fast-approaching generations will know nothing of you at all. Reproducing just to spread your name is selfish, and it will not benefit you whatsoever.

Punishment

There are various effective ways to deal with punishing children for undesirable behavior. Below is a simple list of cause and effect.

Child touching items not meant to be touched (For example, a trash can)- Have the child wear a shock collar. Calmly but firmly instruct the child not to touch the trash can. If it disobeys, shock the child. Adjust shock levels/frequency as needed.

Screaming or crying continuously- After discovering the child actually has what it needs, invest in aircraft earplugs. You won't even know what's going on around you. Before you know it, the child will discover that nagging in an ungodly fashion is not how to achieve results.

Baby talk- This form of communication is unacceptable. You must speak to them like adults. This will result in them being at the top of their class when attending school. You are not to reward them with understanding such horrid communication.

Physical abuse- Children often physically abuse other humans and animals. The only answer to this is reaping what you sow. Place in an electrified cage until they realize what they've done.

Satan- If they choose to partake in Satanic rituals, your only choice is to put them up for adoption. You will join the crowd of realization that you never even actually wanted a child. However, if you are a Satanist, the child will rebelliously join Christianity. The same effect should follow.

This chapter alone is proof that you cannot handle owning a child. Torture is an effective means of punishment, but it may seem (and may be) the only way to achieve results in child raising. Let's be honest- how effective is being kind and mild? It simply isn't. At this point, your only option is to put it up for adoption and hope it does not destroy the lives of other children or adults in the adoption center.

Crime Child Zodiac

Use this guide to discover what type of adult your child will become. They will naturally have these tendencies. Focusing on such flaws will enable you to try to steer them in the correct direction.

What time of crime child do you own? Hopefully not a severe one. There is no escaping a flawed result, and limited actions can be taken. Your Satanic spawn will do whatever they want. At least this guide will show you what they will become in the future.

Hopefully, this only applies to your adult child and they do not begin taking part in these activities as a child.

Gold Digger

January 20- February 18

There's nothing quite like using your body for material gain. If this is your child's zodiac, we all feel sorry for you. Their rachet ways will be evident for the world to see. It puts a bad mark on your family name.

Unfortunately, this type of person will transform into a gold digger regardless of the lifestyle they may have grown up in. They could be born into riches, it doesn't matter. Once they see that gold they just can't stop digging.

To prevent this disease, avoid showing jewelry to your child. Such a sight will activate their innate slank nature. Expensive vehicles can also trigger them. It is nearly impossible to shield them from the view of riches. That is why this condition is mostly unpreventable.

If you are looking to relinquish your child, the best option is to give them to an Amish family. Luckily this type of lifestyle can put their disease into remission.

You can give this type of child gifts on birthdays and holidays, but you must be cautious. Avoid giving them anything shiny. Objects with shine increases their hunger for more material things.

Swindler

February 19- March 20

The Swindler is known to be asking for favors or objects quite often. You will never see a promised return favor or return of your item. This zodiac is opportunistic and will use you as much as you let them.

They are naturally magnetized to anything that says the word "Free" on it. This will drive them to get as much of it as they can. When they see a sign saying "Buy one get one free", they think it's all free.

To encapsulate all Swindlers in any given area, you will have to build a large corral with a ramp over it. Display a large sign saying "Free" over it. In no time, just like cattle to the slaughter they will pile into the enclosure. You will have a group of the sorriest humans you've ever seen. What to do with them from that point is up to your discretion.

To prevent bad behavior in this zodiac, you will need to make them work for everything they have. No presents should be given on the holidays. If they want a meal, they should at least run five miles on a treadmill in order to achieve it. This mindset will prevent the swindling type.

The careless Swindler does not care at all about family or their needs. Be prepared to not only have to pay to raise them, but also pay for your own retirement home because they won't help you when you're senile either.

Sodomy Gang Leader

March 21- April 19

You will want to be very cautious if your child bears this ungodly zodiac. While they may be street-smart in general, they are a little too bossy for their own good.

The first signs of this type include selfish behavior in the forms of relationship status. If a couple is dating, they want control over it. In the meantime, they will be doing whatever they can to destroy the relationships of others so they can get a piece of that ass.

As a teenager, they will begin to form gangs. Everyone below them in the gang is subject to their will. Luckily for the gang members, your offspring will often provide for them in other ways as payment of their service. They will probably have substantial drug money to pay for housing for them.

By the time they reach adulthood, they will have so many tattoos that you will not be able to determine what species they are. It is a status symbol that ensures they can own all of the other followers. As a result, other gang members will automatically bend over when this zodiac approaches. You know what happens next.

Prevent this behavior by not smoking around your child and not enabling them to smoke either. Your incompetent child abuse will result in them resorting to their natural ways of wishing to become the Ultimate Sodomy Gang Leader of all time.

Specialized Arsonist

April 20- May 20

Does your child have an eye for flames? This is a tell-tale sign of a future arsonist. They will be lighting candles wherever they can. Their affinity will be used in all sorts of opposition throughout their life depending on their anger level. From burning your personal belongings, to burning the world.

Keep this zodiac child away from bonfires. If they are exposed to it, their eyes will light up and you will see the Evil Eye appear in their pupils. If you ever reach this point, it's over. They will burn everything in sight to achieve global domination.

The best career for this type of individual would be a fire fighter. They will be able to view immense fires constantly. It will satisfy their needs and they will be doing a good deed for the community at the same time. Otherwise, they will raise hell to the earth and destroy it.

Take for example, welders. This trade tends to have a natural addition to flames. Although they get to work with flames daily, the temptation to overuse is imminent. They will almost always burn everything around the area they are supposed to weld in order to pleasure their inner desires.

Keep your child swimming in a pool constantly in order to keep their evil ways at bay. It will distract them from thinking about fire.

Bioweapon Researcher

May 21- June 20

This type of child will have an above-average intelligence. The problem is that they will use it for evil. Prevent them from getting a 'higher education' on biology and chemistry. Their desire to do so is a sure sign of their attempts at this type of career field.

Coronavirus? More like a virus patented with your child's name on it. Don't let them be a globalist tool. As a child, they're under your control and you shouldn't let them get out of hand. The well-being of the world's population is in your hands if you have a child with this zodiac.

A possible future Bioweapon Researcher will have a natural addiction to needles, experiments, and illnesses. They will begin to perform experiments in the crib. Don't place any lab items within their reach. They will reach for lab coats, beakers, and unknown substances.

"Mommy I want to work in a Bioweapon Lab". You know this phrase all too well. Educate them while they are young and don't let them join the dark side. If needed, you may place them in a cage with experimental animals. They will be able to understand the damage of experimentation and hopefully withdraw from the thought unless they are truly evil inside.

Cattle Prodder

June 21- July 22

Who doesn't like animals? Your child certainly enjoys them. They have an affinity for torture by nature. They both enjoy being tortured and inflicting it on others. It just so happens that animals are often more vulnerable to abuse.

Upon reaching adulthood, your child will do what they can to get into the farming business. It will be kind of a strange angle though. They will focus on areas of farming such as animal slaughter and other areas of animal 'care'. Meanwhile, they are doing everything they can to secretly abuse animals.

Keep an eye on this type during their childhood. They will have a tendency to hurt the family pet. Small animals will be the target at first, and then they will graduate to large animals and finally, humans. Yes, the cattle prodder eventually becomes a murderer if allowed to resume their abusive activities.

This zodiac has their own ultimate fantasy. They wish to be inside a large field full of helpless cattle that are all tied down. They want to have an adjustable cattle prodder electrification device that is able to shock the shit out of the animals. Such a scenario is heaven to this personality type.

Prevent this behavior by not allowing them alone time with animals, or simply not having kids at all.

Shitty Bitchy

July 23- August 22

This type doesn't quite fit in with the others. Neither did they fit in with anything or anyone when they were a child. This causes bitter resentment. Because of this, they can sometimes be among the most dangerous of criminals.

A sure sign of a juvenile shitty bitchy is not being able to handle losing games or on the receiving end of mildly negative situations. They will flip out and make an embarrassing scene of themselves before they will act like an adult.

When they are angered, they will resort to brutal murder over losing a game of checkers. They cannot accept the thought of being wrong or losing. This individual is also often seen robbing others over jealousy or other petty reasons.

Prison is their second home. They will have so many face tattoos that you won't recognize them anymore. After adulthood, their face will twist permanently into a wretched witch face. If only they could cast spells, they would. But their intelligence level does not reach that high to perform witchcraft.

Prevent this state of mind in this child by not having more children. If there's no one to compete with, there's no one to fight over and hate. Forcing them to be alone is the best thing you can do for them.

Stank Weed

August 23- September 22

This may be among the most easily raised of all children. They will grow up as an overall easy-going and relaxed individual. However, a downside to this personality is their lack of personal hygiene. They can go for weeks without bathing. Luckily, the smell of a special herb can help disguise their sheer stank.

Preventing this type of behavior consists of keeping them clean constantly and shielding them from herb exposure. Their childhood association should only consist of those who have extremely active lifestyles. Perhaps, these measures will encourage them to actually work a job in their life.

The Stank Weed is generally a very giving person. They will share whatever they have, but they don't have much. Their favorite hangout area of choice is underneath bridges. If you join them here, they will welcome you without question. They may even be able to aid you in learning graffiti.

If you are a parent of this individual, you'll find that they never want to move out. You will have to force them to move out of the home. Nobody wants to be in a relationship with them either, so you won't get lucky enough for them to go off and go live with a mate. They would often rather be homeless than work a job.

Freemason

September 23- October 22

The first sign of a budding Freemason is their naturally secretive behavior. They're always the quiet type. It is a peaceful child, but an ominous one. What could they be plotting? It is always a mystery. Sometimes their plans could come to fruition quickly, or other times they may be long term plots to change things all around them years ahead of time. Such plots will affect you directly; so, you must watch them closely.

You may have to administer truth serum to determine whether your child has joined the illuminati. This is the only way to know the truth. In school, they will try to form secret groups and keep pacts. Such behavior is proof that children are not actually innocent.

Luckily, upon adulthood this type tends to enter into rather successful careers. However, their family always wonders about what they are actually involved in. They'll never know, unless the child is subject to torture or other similar means.

In relationships, they can tend to have trust problems because their partner is not let in on their secret lifestyle. Divorce is common and reoccurring. They will come back to you for comfort, but in the end will still have to be at arm's length because of the secret society they chose to live their life in.

Porch Pirate

October 23- November 21

This zodiac seems to have no moral compass whatsoever. The horrid signs will show up upon early childhood. One example is the attendance of a funeral. Upon reaching the gravesite, your child can be seen in the background stealing fake flowers from other graves.

When reaching adulthood, they will steal everything they can. It is in their blood. They will not be able to resist a single package on someone's porch. If there is not a package present, they will even steal the trash out of someone's trashcan.

The only remedy for this behavior is slapping the absolute dog shit out of them each time they steal something. Eventually, they will learn such actions are unsatisfactory. It will take a few times because they are not intelligent.

There is one solid way to do away with this type of individual. Set them up with a trap. Put a package on your porch and a cage that encloses around them upon picking up the package. Then, execution can follow.

If you are a parent, execution is probably not preferable. In this case, you can place the cage in the yard and feed them food and water until they die of old age. They are otherwise good for nothing at all.

Crypto Thief

November 22- December 21

You will hope that your child is a crypto thief. This equivalates to endless riches in real life money. Despite their selfish desires, they will have so much money that they can't think of anyone else to shave some of it off to except their own parents. Get ready to retire.

Bitcoin is the go-to currency for this child. They will begin learning about it at a young age. Encourage digital education. Without further teaching, they will begin to see the dark side on their own. Upon reaching adulthood, they will be able to afford a brand-new car and multiple homes. Sometimes, they may not admit their riches to their family.

A good indication of hidden riches is manifested gains. You will notice the accumulation of expensive items suddenly. They may claim they are making payments, but that couldn't be further from the truth. They are in fact rich and may not wish to share it at the time.

The only way to get on the same level is to learn crypto currency yourself. This may cause them to open up to you about what they are actually doing.

If you wish to prevent this way of life in your child, you must shield them from all computers and technology.

Crisis Actor

December 22- January 19

What a familiar face! We've seen them at the warzone. No wait, we saw them at the shooting on television! That's right, your child is a star. Sadly, they are not a star with any kind of honor. Their name will be scrubbed from the system once a few jobs are done.

While your child may not have broken any actual laws, they broke humanity's law of respect in everyone else's eyes. Congratulations, your offspring is a tool of the New World Order. It doesn't get much lower than this.

There is a surefire way to prevent this type of behavior. Fixate a back brace to your child to ensure their posture is in an upright position. This will successfully prevent boot-licking. You will be able to observe their focus, and see whether they are staring at other individuals' shoes. Eventually, they can overcome the habit.

Having integrity does not come natural for this child. They are followers and have no chance of really succeeding in life. If their crisis actor career does not take off, they will often resort to becoming an underpaid CEO at a department store.

In childhood, the first signs you will see of them transforming into a crisis actor is lying about basic topics. Keep them on track by having them practice their archery on the illuminati symbol.

References

Centers for Disease Control and Prevention. (2020, September 1). *How are Children Different from Adults?* Retrieved from Centers for Disease Control and Prevention: https://www.cdc.gov/childrenindisasters/differences.html

Centers for Disease Control and Prevention. (2021, November 22). *CDCs Abortion Surveillance System FAQs*. Retrieved from Centers for Disease Control and Prevention: https://www.cdc.gov/reproductivehealth/data_stats/abortion.htm

Lifelong Adoptions. (n.d.). *ADOPTION STATISTICS*. Retrieved from Lifelong Adoptions: https://www.lifelongadoptions.com/adoption-statistics

Parker, T. (2022, January 9). *The Cost of Raising a Child in the United States*. Retrieved from Investopedia: https://www.investopedia.com/articles/personal-finance/090415/cost-raising-child-america.asp#:~:text=According%20to%20the%20U.S.%20Department,could%20be%20estimated%20at%20%24272%2C049.

Webber, J. (2019, August 28). *New Data Reveals Just How Much Sleep New Parents Are Losing Nightly*. Retrieved from Healthline: https://www.healthline.com/health/parenting/new-parent-sleep-study#This-too-shall-pass

www.ingramcontent.com/pod-product-compliance
Lightning Source LLC
Chambersburg PA
CBHW071800020426
42331CB00008B/2340